DSC SPEED READS

COMMUNICATIONS

Staff Forums

Dean Renshaw

Published by the Directory of Social Change (Registered Charity no. 800517 in England and Wales)

Office: Suite 103, 1 Old Hall Street, Liverpool L3 9HG

Tel: 020 4526 5995

Visit www.dsc.org.uk to find out more about our books, subscription funding website and training events. You can also sign up for e-newsletters so that you're always the first to hear about what's new.

The publisher welcomes suggestions and comments that will help to inform and improve future versions of this and all of our titles. Please give us your feedback by emailing publications@dsc.org.uk

It should be understood that this publication is intended for guidance only and is not a substitute for professional advice. No responsibility for loss occasioned as a result of any person acting or refraining from acting can be accepted by the author or publisher.

Print and digital editions first published 2022

Copyright © Directory of Social Change 2022

All rights reserved. No part of the printed version of this book may be stored in a retrieval system or reproduced in any form whatsoever without prior permission in writing from the publisher. This book is sold subject to the condition that it shall not, by way of trade or otherwise, be lent, re-sold, hired out or otherwise circulated without the publisher's prior permission in any form of binding or cover other than that in which it is published, and without a similar condition including this condition being imposed on the subsequent purchaser.

The digital version of this publication may only be stored in a retrieval system for personal use. No part may be edited, amended, extracted or reproduced in any form whatsoever. It may not be distributed or made available to others without prior permission in writing from the publisher.

The publisher and author have made every effort to contact copyright holders. If anyone believes that their copyright material has not been correctly acknowledged, please contact the publisher, who will be pleased to rectify the omission.

The moral right of the author has been asserted in accordance with the Copyrights, Designs and Patents Act 1988.

ISBN 978 1 78482 098 5 (print edition)
ISBN 978 1 78482 099 2 (digital edition)

British Library Cataloguing in Publication Data
A catalogue record for this book is available from the British Library

Cover and text design by Kate Griffith
Printed and bound in the UK by Martins the Printers, Berwick upon Tweed

Contents

Introduction

Chapter 1: **Why have a staff forum?**   **5**
- The very beginning   5
- Why you need staff forums   6
- What are staff forums for?   7
- What are staff forums not for?   8

Chapter 2: **Constituting the forum**   **10**
- Getting started   10
- Writing the rules   11
- Staff forum representatives   14
- Who to invite   15
- Digital or in-person staff forums   16

Chapter 3: **Before the meeting**   **18**
- Scheduling   18
- Submitting items for discussion   19
- Agendas   20

Chapter 4: **On the day**   **21**
- Final preparations   21
- Running the staff forum meeting   22

Chapter 5: **After the meeting**   **26**
- Preparing notes and feedback   26
- Giving feedback   27
- Receiving feedback   27
- What if your senior leader disagrees?   28
- Planning for the next staff forum meeting   28

Chapter 6: **Troubleshooting**   **29**
- Common issues   29
- Rome wasn't built in a day   32

Introduction

Who will this book help?

This book is a guide for staff and senior leaders on how to set up and maintain a staff forum – a series of peer-powered meetings that give staff the time and space to raise any issues that may be affecting their working lives.

What will it give you?

This book will give you the skills and knowledge to set up and run staff forums. It will take you through the key steps all the way from starting to consider why you should have staff forums, to the things you'll need to do in advance of the staff forum meeting, through to the preparations needed on the day of the meeting and what needs to be done afterwards to keep staff forums going.

Chapter 1

Why have a staff forum?

This chapter looks at what staff forums are, why you need them, what they can be used for and what they should not be used for.

The very beginning

According to one of the many legends of Ancient Rome, two warring kings met in a marshy valley, ended their war and formed an alliance. Over time, this location grew into the Roman Forum, a space for a range of social, political and religious activities, such as meetings, elections and funerals. It was one of the most important places in Ancient Rome.

There's a reason why today we call the meetings described in this book staff forums. Staff forums, much like the Roman Forum, are about giving a voice – in this case to staff.

What are staff forums?

Staff forums are a series of regular meetings that are designed and delivered by staff, for staff. They are an opportunity for colleagues to discuss things that are happening at work and to raise any issues that may be affecting them in a safe and positive environment, which can then be fed back to a senior leader (or a group of senior leaders) within your organisation. Staff forums are typically held without managers or directors, although this may vary depending on the organisation. For example, a particularly large organisation may choose to include middle management positions but not senior leaders.

The basic structure of staff forums is simple and consists of two parts: the meeting of staff (the forum itself) and the feedback session with a senior leader. Ideally, you want the feedback to go directly to the chief executive but, depending on the size and structure of your organisation, another member of your leadership team may be more appropriate, or you could be providing feedback to multiple members of your leadership team. For simplicity, in this Speed Read, we'll refer to the person (or people) receiving the feedback as the senior leader.

Staff forums can have many different names, including staff consultations, employee forums and staff assemblies, but they all operate similarly.

Staff forums can be designed to suit the structure and nature of your organisation. For example, if your organisation is large, you may want to have a few different staff forums for individual teams.

The topics covered in a staff forum can be broad; you could be having discussions about how you would like to improve equality, equity, diversity and inclusion in your workplace, or you could be deciding on the best way to celebrate your colleagues' birthdays.

Why you need staff forums

In any organisation, communication is always going to be one of the most important considerations to keep things running smoothly. Think of staff forums as a way of ensuring that there's good communication circulating throughout your organisation. They're also an opportunity to raise or explore the topics that don't quite belong in your other channels of communication and allows them to be brought to the attention of the senior leader.

Ideally, staff will already have methods and procedures in place for when they talk to line managers, such as regular one-to-one meetings. But there will be times when these usual routes aren't sufficient. There may be issues that some staff feel are relatively unimportant on a singular basis but, collectively, they may reflect a trend in thinking across staff and become more worthy of attention.

If you're the senior leader, you want your staff to be communicating well. It will benefit both the staff and the leadership team to have a range of methods in place for communication throughout the organisation, because it reduces the chances of things falling through the cracks and helps staff to feel that their leadership team is listening.

What are staff forums for?

Almost anything! Here are just a few examples of what you could discuss at your staff forum:

- Creating new policies at your organisation or adjusting existing ones.
- Clarification of policies at your organisation, such as webcam etiquette while working from home.
- Things your leadership team could do to support staff well-being.
- Things that the staff could do differently to promote environmental sustainability in the workplace.
- Any personal development opportunities, such as online courses, which you think would be useful to share.

It doesn't just have to be about work either. You could also discuss:

- Social events that you could hold outside working hours.
- TV, film, book, music or podcast recommendations.

- Videos of talks or seminars on relevant topics. TED Talks are a great resource for this, and you could even hold your own TED Talks on topics that the staff are interested in.

What are staff forums not for?

There's a good reason why staff forums have so far been described as a place where you can discuss *almost* anything. While they provide an opportunity to talk about a huge range of issues and topics, ranging from trivial to important, there are certain things that staff forums must not be used for. If you are running the staff forum, then you must be prepared to veto topics or suggestions that are not suitable.

> **Where next?**
> Informing and consulting your employees about workplace matters
>
> *www.acas.org.uk/ informing-and- consulting-with- your-employees- about-workplace- matters*

Legal obligations

Senior leaders need to be aware that staff forums must not be used to replace any sort of legal obligation to consult staff – this should be a separate process.

> **Where next?**
> *www.gov.uk/informing- consulting-employees- law*

In the UK, certain situations require employers to inform and consult staff, such as on health and safety issues or if an employer is selling a business. These may change over time, and the exact process required may vary depending on which country of the UK you're in, so make sure to check what your legal obligations are.

Existing communication channels

Staff forums should not replace any existing communication in your organisation. If you're a member of staff, you should still be having regular meetings with your line manager and use those meetings to talk about what's important to you (even if the same topic is going to be discussed at a staff forum).

Grievances or complaints about staff

There may be complaints or grievances in your organisation concerning specific members of staff. A staff forum is not the appropriate place to discuss these issues and it's the role of the staff forum lead to reject this if it comes up and to direct staff to the appropriate channels for grievances and complaints. You should have a complaints and/or grievance policy in place for your organisation. If you don't, make one.

Case study

'When we initially launched our staff forum, the CEO spoke about it at an All Teams Call, so everyone understood what it was and why it was important. We then asked for volunteers to join the forum from across as many departments as possible. We also have HR and trade union representatives on the forum, and it's chaired by our CEO. The Staff Forum Representatives gather input, feedback and questions from their department teams and bring these to the monthly forum meetings for wider discussion.

We ask for agenda items in advance, so everyone can contribute. Each meeting, the CEO will provide an opening update on any key issues or initiatives and answer any questions raised. We discuss the agenda items as a group and share our input. The Staff Forum Representatives then take back the discussions points and updates and share them with their teams. The staff forum is important as part of our overall employee communications and engagement strategy.'

Jill Burgess, Interim Head of HR, Volunteering Matters

Chapter 2

Constituting the forum

This chapter explains how to constitute and develop your staff forum.

Getting started

The person running the staff forum is the staff forum lead. This doesn't have to be just one person: you could have an entire team of people running your staff forum, you may decide to have multiple staff forums (each with a separate lead) or you may be taking turns to share the responsibility.

This first stage of setting up the forum should be a conversation between the staff forum lead and the senior leader. It's important to clearly outline and understand the roles that you will all play in the staff forum.

If you're the senior leader, your role is to listen to the feedback from your staff forum and respond to it. You should let the staff forum lead know what action you're going to take because of the feedback. You may, of course, decide that no action is needed; however, you should still explain the reason why you're not going to do anything.

Below is a short checklist of the things that the staff forum lead will be required to do.

> **Responsibilities of the staff forum lead**
> - Scheduling staff forum meetings
> - Writing the agendas for staff forum meetings
> - Vetoing inappropriate topics and helping people to find the right channel to deal with them
> - Chairing staff forum meetings
> - Scheduling feedback sessions with your senior leader
> - Sharing feedback with the senior leader
> - Sharing any actions your senior leader took (or reasons why no action was taken) because of staff forums

By the end of this conversation between the staff forum lead and the senior leader, you should be clear about what your respective roles are, understand what the staff forum will and will not be used for and agree on the timings for the staff forum meetings and follow-up feedback sessions. An essential part of this conversation is creating a set of rules for your staff forum, which is covered in the following section.

Writing the rules

As part of the early conversation between the senior leader and the staff forum lead, you'll want to establish the rules for your staff forum. This is going to be one of the most important things that you will do together. A solid set of rules will aid you in running the staff forum and help your colleagues to understand what is expected of them in the process.

Below are a few examples of rules you could incorporate into your staff forum. But remember that every staff forum is unique, so you have the freedom to play around with the rules to come up with something that works for your organisation.

Rules about respect

If attendees aren't respectful of each other, people won't enjoy the meetings and, eventually, they'll stop coming altogether. Rules around respect could include:

- When somebody is talking at the staff forum meeting, everyone should be listening.
- Don't interrupt; wait for your turn to speak.
- Arrive at the staff forum meeting on time.
- The chair should finish the staff forum meeting on time.

Rules on anonymity

You won't be able to guarantee that everyone's anonymous at the staff forum meeting (you'll all be talking to each other and know who said what); however, you can make sure that colleagues aren't identified outside the meeting and ensure anonymity that way.

If you include a rule on anonymity, follow it throughout the entire process. This means that even when you're sharing feedback with the senior leader, you don't identify anyone at that stage unless that person permitted you.

A note of caution: anonymity can become difficult to manage when there's a specific issue that needs resolving. If the staff forum lead is giving feedback to the senior leader and says that 'someone' has a problem with a certain issue, it's not very useful to the senior leader and there may be very little they can do to solve the problem. Who has an issue with it? Is it a problem for a certain team? Is it a specific manager causing the problem?

On the other hand, anonymity can be very useful in staff forums. Some staff are naturally shy and others may have medical conditions such as social anxiety that make them hesitant to share or discuss things openly. It may be the case that some staff want to raise an issue but don't want to share specific details.

For example, a member of staff might want to suggest having a 'faith day' off for people of different faiths, but they don't want to discuss their religion at work.

Try putting the question of anonymity in staff forums as one of the items to discuss in your first staff forum meeting. Not only will it help to illustrate how staff forums work and how they can bring about change, you'll also then have a rule on anonymity that your colleagues have agreed on.

Keep staff forums positive

Another rule to consider is how you can make the staff forum a positive environment – welcoming, friendly and something that staff look forward to participating in. The last thing you want is for your staff forums to become a place where people are constantly criticising things and complaining about others. To incorporate positivity in your staff forum, consider having rules like 'focus on what we can do to improve things and not on what's gone wrong' or 'the staff forum isn't the place to complain about things'.

Transparency

Staff forums should be transparent. The senior leaders who are not invited to the staff forum meetings should still be able to find out when the meetings are, and the agendas and meeting notes should be stored somewhere where everyone in the organisation can access them, such as on a shared network drive. This lets senior leaders know that the staff forums are run well and can give them confidence in the process.

If you incorporate a rule on anonymity in your staff forum, you may be wondering how you can uphold this rule and keep your staff forum transparent. The rule on transparency should relate to the topics discussed and the staff forum process itself – not to the staff attending the staff forum meeting.

Write up your rules

The rules should be easy to find and easy to read. Write up your rules and put them somewhere where all staff can access them quickly, such as on a shared network drive.

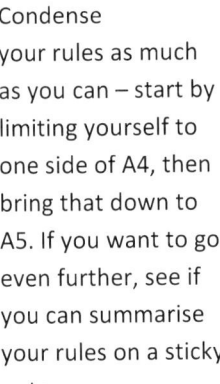

Top tip
Condense your rules as much as you can – start by limiting yourself to one side of A4, then bring that down to A5. If you want to go even further, see if you can summarise your rules on a sticky note.

Staff forum representatives

Staff forum representatives are members of staff who help the staff forum lead to organise and run the forum. They will assist with collecting items for the staff forum agenda from colleagues, running the discussions in the staff forum meeting and sharing the feedback with the senior leader.

Aside from being an aid to the staff forum lead, staff forum representatives are also a good way to ensure that there's continuity in your staff forum. If the staff forum lead is ill or unavailable, then a staff forum representative could chair the staff forum. And if the staff forum lead leaves your organisation, one of the staff forum representatives will already have the skills and experience to take over, and you can keep your staff forum going with minimal disruption.

The exact number of staff forum representatives will vary according to your organisation. You could start with one staff forum representative for every five members of staff attending – this would mean that when you run a staff forum and you go into smaller groups to discuss things, your staff forum representatives will be running a group of about five people.

You may also want to consider how you'll appoint staff forum representatives. Some organisations rely on people who have volunteered for the role, but you could also hold elections for staff forum representatives for a limited term, so that different colleagues get some experience.

You may also want to bear in mind equality, equity, diversity and inclusion considerations – do your staff forum representatives reflect the make-up of your organisation's staff?

Who to invite

Another thing you'll need to consider is who exactly should attend the staff forum meetings. This is going to vary a lot between organisations, but one suggestion would be that the staff forum should only be for members of staff who are not senior leaders.

There are two reasons for this. Firstly, staff forums shouldn't replace any of the usual responsibilities or discussions between line managers and staff, so staff will still be having their regular catch-ups and one-to-ones with managers where they can raise anything that their manager can help them with. Secondly, staff need to feel comfortable that they can raise almost any issue at staff forums, and it's always going to be easier to discuss issues among peers.

> **Top tip**
> Ensure you have representation from across the organisation on the forum, including any existing trade union representation.
>
> **Jill Burgess, Interim Head of HR, Volunteering Matters**

This may not be practical in your organisation, of course. In a particularly large organisation, you may have varying levels of management, and so it may be appropriate to include middle or even senior managers in the staff forum. Depending on the size and structure of your organisation, you may decide to run a separate staff forum for each team or department.

There are no set rules for how many people should be attending staff forum meetings, but the things you discuss should feel like conversations and not lectures – if you notice that your staff forum is too big for everyone to voice their views, then it is probably time to split it up into smaller groups.

If you do decide to run multiple staff forums, consider how you'll co-ordinate them all. For example, will you still have one staff forum lead running each staff forum meeting or will you need multiple people who will work together to prepare the feedback for the senior leader?

Digital or in-person staff forums

Digital staff forums

Video conferencing software allows you to hold staff forums almost anywhere. If you're running a digital staff forum, spend some time investigating what software you'll be using. You'll want to find something easy to use for everyone and something that allows you to use 'breakout rooms' (a function that lets you divide your meeting into separate smaller groups).

In-person staff forums

If you're holding your staff forum in person, you'll need to find an appropriate space to hold it such as a meeting room.

You may need to hire a space if you don't have meeting rooms or if your meeting rooms aren't suitable (for example, too small or of limited availability). Make sure it's big enough for everyone to be comfortable and that it's easy to access for everybody attending. For example, is it somewhere that can be easily accessed by public transport?

When you're running the staff forum meeting itself, you won't be able to use breakout rooms in the same way as with a digital staff forum meeting, but you can replicate this by dividing the group up into smaller clusters of people. Remember that you may need a large meeting room to do this, as a small meeting room may get too cramped and noisy when the different groups are talking.

Which is better?

Digital staff forums are more convenient: people don't have to travel, and you can have people from all over the world attending easily. But think carefully about the technology that you choose to make sure that everybody is comfortable and able to use it well.

In-person staff forums have more of a social benefit, you can socialise before and after the meeting, and technical difficulties won't be as disruptive as they would be in digital staff forums. Some staff may also find it easier to contribute face-to-face rather than on a screen. But staff will have to travel somewhere, which can be expensive or time-consuming. You could also unintentionally exclude staff who have other commitments, such as caring responsibilities, and therefore can't travel to staff forum meetings.

Communicate with each other to see which approach you think would work best and then try it. You can always change the way you run your staff forum later, and you don't have to stick to one or the other. You could also do a mixture of in-person and digital staff forums throughout the year.

> **Top tip**
>
> If you're hosting a digital staff forum, consider if online forums will be recorded and, if they aren't anonymous forums, will the recordings be shared with all staff?
>
> **Karen Timbrell, Human Resources Support Officer, WCVA**

Chapter 3

Before the meeting

This chapter covers the things you need to do before the staff forum meeting: finding the right time, gathering agenda items and writing the agenda.

Top tip

When scheduling the staff forum, choose the dates yourself and share them well in advance rather than trying to agree with everyone first. However, try to avoid clashes with school holidays, product or report launches and important meetings when staff may be busy.

Scheduling

Even in small organisations, finding a time that works for all staff is going to be tricky.

Plan the dates for all your staff forum meetings for the coming 12 months at the beginning of the year so that staff have plenty of notice and can organise other events around them. Send invitations out to make sure that everyone has each staff forum meeting in their calendar. One suggestion would be to start by scheduling quarterly meetings. If you need more (or fewer) meetings, you can adjust the number later.

At the same time, you'll want to schedule your feedback sessions with the senior leader. Make these at least one week after the staff forum meeting, because staff will need some time to read the notes from your staff forum meeting and may have additional suggestions or further comments to take to the senior leader.

If you're the senior leader, try to be aware of when the staff forum meetings are and promote them. At this stage of the process, your role is very hands-off, but that doesn't mean you're not allowed to talk about it. Encourage staff to attend and avoid scheduling other meetings at the same time as staff forums take place if you can.

Submitting items for discussion

You'll want to make sure that you offer a few different ways to submit items for the agenda for your staff forums. Here are a few examples of how staff could suggest items for the agenda:

- Talk to the staff forum lead or one of the staff forum representatives.
- Use existing communication platforms you have in your workplace that allow you to post topics in channels or group chats.
- Create a dedicated email inbox at your organisation for staff forum and email suggestions there.
- Leave a note in a physical post box in your office.

You may also want to add a method of submitting items anonymously. This can be useful for sensitive topics or for topics that staff aren't comfortable raising for any reason. An anonymous method of submitting items can be created using online survey tools.

> **Where next?**
> Make a free anonymous survey
> www.google.co.uk/forms/about

If you're gathering items for the staff forum and someone suggests an unsuitable topic, then politely let them know why you won't be including it and offer an alternative route to help with the issue they raised. For example, if somebody submits an item that says their workload is too much, tell the person that their suggestion isn't suitable for the staff forum but that their line manager would be the best person to talk to in the first instance.

When you have chosen and set up your methods for submitting items, promote them regularly to your colleagues. Staff should always know how they can contribute to the agenda. Send reminder emails about a month and then two weeks before the staff forum meeting to let colleagues know that staff forum is coming up and that they can submit any topics they would like to discuss at the meeting.

Agendas

Writing an agenda for each staff forum is vital. The agenda should have:

- **The introduction** to the staff forum, which will include a recap of what the staff forum is and isn't for, the rules, who the staff forum representatives are and what they'll be doing in the staff forum meeting.
- **The items** to be discussed and how you'll discuss them (for example, in breakout rooms or smaller groups in a physical meeting).

A week before the staff forum meeting, the staff forum lead should write a draft agenda and share it with all the staff attending, giving them the opportunity to adjust the agenda. Certain topics may need clarification, for example if the staff forum lead has misunderstood an item that was submitted.

Include timings in your agenda to help you run the meeting. Not all topics will require the same amount of time to discuss. For example, the topic of 'should we buy birthday cakes?' likely won't take as long as 'should we do more around our equality, equity, diversity and inclusion policies?'.

Some topics in the agenda can be quite broad, so add prompts to the agenda too. These are short questions that staff can use to guide the discussion. For example, if your agenda item is 'could we do more for the environment at work?', then some of your prompts could be:

- What do we already do for the environment at work?
- What could we do better?
- What do other organisations do for the environment at work?
- Could we buy alternative products, like recycled paper?
- Should we stop using plastic cups at the water cooler?

Chapter 4

On the day

This chapter looks at the things you need to do on the day of the staff forum meeting: the final preparations, how to run the session and the role of the staff forum lead and representatives.

Final preparations

It's the day of your staff forum meeting. As the staff forum lead, you're most likely (but not necessarily always) going to be the chair of the staff forum meeting, so it's important to be prepared. Check your agenda – have there been any adjustments or suggestions to change it? If you can make those changes, do so – but don't substantially alter the agenda on the day. If there are new items, you could add them in if there's time; however, if your agenda is already full, any new items would have to wait until the next staff forum. If anything is added to the agenda, let everyone know about it as soon as you can rather than letting people discover it for the first time in the staff forum meeting itself.

Before the meeting, the staff forum lead should go over the rules again to remind themselves of what exactly the rules are. It may have been a few months since the last staff forum meeting, so it's useful to do this as a refresher.

On the day

If someone informs you that they can't attend, thank them for letting you know and ask them if there's anything they were going to say in the meeting. Just because someone can't make it to the meeting doesn't mean that they can't contribute. The staff forum lead can relay the thoughts of that person in the meeting.

Running the staff forum meeting

> **Top tip**
> The themes and outcomes of the staff forum must be led by the staff (not by managers and their desires).
>
> **George Knight, Training Consultant, DSC**

The meeting has started. Regular meeting conventions should apply to staff forums too (remind colleagues of this), so if people are slow to join the meeting or arrive in person, you can give them a few minutes if time allows, but try not to stray too far from the timings in the agenda.

Thank everyone for coming and tell everyone what the rules are and what the staff forum should and shouldn't be used for. Open *every* staff forum meeting with the rules. It may seem needlessly repetitive, but the rules are important. It's a good idea to ask people if they have any questions about them.

Once the rules are out of the way, briefly go over the topics that you'll discuss. Don't go into too much depth at this stage, but everyone should have a good idea of what they'll be talking about – don't assume that everyone has read the agenda.

Now split everyone up into smaller groups. Each group will be run by a staff forum representative. If you're meeting in person, ask people to sit together. If you're doing this digitally, set up breakout rooms in the software you're using to run the staff

> **Where next?**
> *Meetings* by Helen Rice and Maria Pemberton (DSC Speed Read)

forum. Try to get a good mix of staff in each breakout room by making groups composed of people from different departments or functions in your organisation, and try to avoid putting people who often work together in the same group so that discussions can have a diverse range of opinions from across your organisation.

Then the actual discussions start. The staff forum lead can run a group along with the staff forum representatives, or they can go around each group and see how things are going, remind everyone of how long they have left on each item and check if anyone needs any help, like clarification on the agenda items.

Staff forum representatives can use the prompts to start the discussion. Try and make sure that everyone's had the chance to speak. Some people are naturally more reserved than others, but it's important to get their opinion too. When you're sharing what you've discussed, it should be representative of everyone in your group. Pay attention to the people who aren't talking, and if somebody hasn't had a chance to contribute, you can ask them directly what they think. You don't want somebody to feel like they've been singled out, though, so instead of saying things like 'you haven't said much' try to prompt them with a simple 'what do you think about this?'. Sometimes the opposite will be true, and a colleague may dominate the conversation to the detriment of other staff. If this happens, you can politely interrupt them by saying things like 'that's a great thought, what do the rest of you think?'.

> **Top tip**
> In an in-person staff forum meeting, it can be tricky to mix people up into different groups. Try to get people to physically move around the room to form new groups rather than grouping people by where they're already sitting.

If you're running your staff forum digitally, the staff forum lead may want to stay in the main meeting room. This means that anybody who's late to the

On the day

meeting can then be assigned to a breakout room, or they can go through the items with the staff forum lead.

When you've discussed each of the items, bring everyone back together. In a digital meeting, close the breakout rooms and return to the main meeting room. The staff forum lead will then ask each staff forum representative to share what they discussed for the first agenda item. Give every staff forum representative the chance to talk about the agenda item before moving on to the next one (as opposed to letting each staff forum representative talk about every agenda item and then moving on to the next staff forum representative). Staff may have additional ideas because of things said in other groups, so finish one agenda item before moving on to the next.

Top tip

Remember that you'll be giving feedback to your senior leader based on the conversations in the staff forum meeting. Request specific examples or ask staff 'what would you like the senior leader to do?'

The staff forum lead should take notes on everything that's discussed. Try to be as comprehensive as you can, and don't paraphrase what somebody says in case you unintentionally misconstrue their opinion or what they said. You should be thinking about exactly what you'll say to your senior leader.

At the end of the staff forum meeting, thank everyone for coming and let them know when you'll write up the notes and share them.

Staff forums – a senior leader's perspective

'Our staff forum at DSC is one of the most useful practices we have. It is entirely owned and run by our staff. They are the ones who set the agendas, although if I or our leadership team want to get a sense of the staff's feelings about something, we can (and often do) ask the Staff Forum Representatives to bring the item to the staff forum meeting and then feed back to us. This doesn't replace more formal consultations and meetings between staff and their line managers but really does enhance the quality of information we need to make good decisions. Frequently, the staff forum will raise something that we haven't even thought about as either being an issue or indeed (and more often!) a good idea that we can implement.

A valuable part of the process is that I meet with the Staff Forum Representatives directly to hear the feedback from the staff and discuss the topics that have been raised. It gives me an opportunity to explain my thinking, the context we are operating in and the challenges we face, as well as to get a direct account of what the staff think the course of action should be and how they would like to support the leadership team to deal with the issue.

These sessions also mean the staff see the leadership team as accessible and willing to listen, and when we can't or won't implement a change or a new idea that they suggest, I have the opportunity to explain my thinking and get their response. I always share the feedback from the staff forum at our leadership team meetings to make sure that we all understand and are aligned behind any actions or decisions we need to make.

A key element of our staff forum's success is that as CEO I actively promote the forum, encourage staff to attend the meetings and talk about how important staff forums are and how much I value the feedback. That means staff feel empowered to participate in the forum and see that it matters. I'm incredibly proud of our staff forum. And it works.'

Debra Allcock Tyler, CEO, DSC

Chapter 5

After the meeting

This chapter looks at what to do after the staff forum meeting: preparing and giving feedback to your senior leader, updating staff and planning for the next meeting.

Preparing notes and feedback

Following a staff forum meeting, write up the notes. It's tempting to put it off, but it's best to do it while the meeting and discussions are fresh in your mind.

Make the notes easy to read and understand, avoid jargon and acronyms – you may know what it all means, but will a new colleague? When you write the notes, make them as clear as you can and try to make sure that what you write reflects what was discussed in the staff forum meeting. Once you have the notes completed, share them with everyone who attended the meeting. Just like with the agenda, you want all staff to have the opportunity to make any notes or add any clarifications.

Remember that nothing at a staff forum is secret, so everybody should be able to find what was discussed easily. Ideally, you'll want to store the notes wherever you store the agenda and the rules.

Giving feedback

The next step is to attend the feedback session with the senior leader. It's useful to also invite the staff forum representatives, as they were directly involved in the discussions at the staff forum meeting, so they'll be able to offer clarifications on what was discussed if the senior leader needs a bit more context or an explanation.

This doesn't have to be a formal meeting and should be more of a conversation between the staff forum lead and representatives and the senior leader.

When giving feedback to your senior leader, present an overview of the topics you discussed, outline any suggested actions or things that the staff would like to see happen, and give examples if you feel that it would make things clearer.

Receiving feedback

If you're the senior leader, the main thing you need to do is listen. You may not agree with the issues raised and the suggestions proposed, and you may have different solutions or compromises, but the important thing is that you are listening to what your staff are telling you and that the staff feel that they are being listened to. This goes a long way in making staff feel that staff forums are a useful way to spend their time at work.

Once you've heard the feedback, tell the staff forum team what you'll be doing about each of these points. Let them know who you'll be talking to and when they can expect to see a result from the feedback.

Of course, you don't have to do whatever the staff forum says you should do. You are the leader and it's your responsibility to make decisions. If you disagree with any of the points made or suggestions offered, explain to the staff forum team why you disagree, so that they can share the reasons with the rest of the staff.

What if your senior leader disagrees?

Sometimes the senior leader will disagree with something discussed at staff forum and not take it any further. This could be for a range of reasons: maybe it's not practical, there are legal obligations to consider or there are financial implications. But that's okay. It's the senior leader's job to lead and make decisions. The important thing is that you feel that your senior leader listened to you and that they are genuinely invested in staff forums. People will always disagree – this isn't a failure but a sign of healthy communication.

The staff forum lead should share this feedback with colleagues too, even if no action will be taken. Tell the staff what the senior leader said and why they disagreed. Some staff may be disappointed with the outcome, especially if they were the ones to raise the agenda item, so it's helpful to always give reasons for the senior leader's decision. Staff forums aren't there to impose rules or decisions – that responsibility lies with the senior leader.

Planning for the next staff forum meeting

Share the feedback from the senior leader with the people who attended the staff forum and let them know what's going to be done (or why no action will be taken). Then it's time to start preparing for the next staff forum meeting. Let staff know when it is and remind them how they can submit agenda items. You've completed this round of the staff forum – congratulations!

Chapter 6

Troubleshooting

This final chapter looks at some of the common issues that can affect staff forums.

Common issues

People aren't attending staff forum meetings

Some people may not participate in staff forums because they think the forums are not important or they don't have the time. Try to encourage people to attend by contacting them directly, either in person or by email, and asking them if there's anything you can do to help. It may be the case that you're unintentionally scheduling the meetings at inconvenient times.

You can always ask the senior leader to promote staff forums. It may encourage colleagues to know that the senior leader endorses staff forums and considers attending the meetings to be good use of work time. If more staff attend, then the feedback from the staff forum meetings will be more representative of what the staff truly think.

Sensitive topics

Don't shy away from sensitive topics just because they might be difficult to talk about. If you know a sensitive topic is going to come up, do some research and get a better understanding of what you'll be talking about. Language is particularly important when discussing sensitive topics, so make sure you're

Troubleshooting

not unintentionally using outdated or offensive language (even if you don't realise that it's offensive). For example, talk about 'people living with mental health conditions' and not 'the mentally ill'.

Gossiping

Stop this as soon as you can by politely but firmly reminding people that staff forum should not be used for complaints or grievances about specific staff and direct them to the appropriate policy in your organisation if necessary. It's understandable – to a degree – for people to moan about their managers, but that's not what a staff forum is for.

There's nothing to discuss

Where next?

Mind offers advice and resources on different types of mindfulness exercise

www.mind.org.uk/inform ation-support/drugs-and-treatments/mindfulness/ mindfulness-exercises-tips

As you approach your staff forum meeting date, you may find that no topics have been suggested. Remind staff how they can submit topics and you'll often find that colleagues start submitting things once they're prompted.

Don't forget that staff forums don't have to be exclusively about issues affecting staff at work. If you have a relatively sparse agenda, you could consider adding a relevant talk (for example, TED Talks on YouTube) or try a mindfulness exercise (which can also be found on YouTube) to wind down the staff forum.

Staff disagree

This is perfectly natural in any healthy relationship, but you want to keep an eye on language like 'you're wrong' or 'that's not how it is', which could lead to more serious arguments. Instead, offer alternatives like 'so you disagree, would it help if you explained your position?'.

Vague discussions

If colleagues are discussing agenda items in vague or confusing ways, ask for clarification on what they mean. If they can't do that, ask for an example that illustrates their point. If you don't understand the point being made, then neither will your senior leader.

Repeated agenda items

Some agenda items may be submitted repeatedly, especially if the senior leader decided not to take any action on it last time. The staff forum lead will need to decide whether to include this again. If it's something staff feel passionate about or if the context around the issue has changed, then it may be worth discussing the item again.

Sometimes this may happen because a member of staff is unaware that it's been raised before — if this happens, you can point your colleague to the meeting notes from the staff forum meeting when this was raised.

However, if issues do come up time and time again, the staff forum lead should veto them from the agenda. This is to ensure that there's time for new agenda items, and so that staff don't feel like they're repeating themselves and wasting their time, which may result in staff no longer attending your staff forums.

Handover guidance

The staff forum lead won't always be around. They may leave the organisation, or they may become ineligible to attend staff forums (for example, if they are promoted to a managerial role in an organisation that excludes line managers from staff forums). Having a handover procedure in place will help to minimise any disruption this causes to staff forums.

The most likely candidates for the next staff forum lead will likely be among the staff forum representatives. They will have worked closely with the staff forum lead and have been involved in the entire process, so they'll know what they need to do. If a staff forum representative wishes to become the next staff forum lead, then the departing staff forum lead should spend some time talking through the role, including what they'll need to do and share any tips the staff forum lead has learned from experience.

Rome wasn't built in a day

One last thing. Whether you're the staff forum lead, a staff forum representative or the senior leader who's receiving the feedback from staff forums, remember that this is a constantly evolving process.

There may be teething issues with technology, or maybe you haven't picked the best time to run a staff forum meeting but try not to worry about it. Over time, as you become more and more comfortable with staff forums, you'll learn these things. You'll have ideas on how you can make staff forums more relevant for your organisation, and you'll tweak things that you think aren't working as well as they should be.

Think back to the Roman Forum when it was founded on that marshy land. It didn't spring into existence fully formed. It grew, slowly and organically. Bits were added, and pieces were removed. It took time to perfect it, and the same is true for staff forums. Rome wasn't built in a day.